Slovakia
HIGH TATRAS
Stephen Platt

www.leveretpublishing.com

Slovakia: High Tatras
First published - January 2024
Published by Leveret Publishing
56 Covent Garden, Cambridge, CB1 2HR, UK

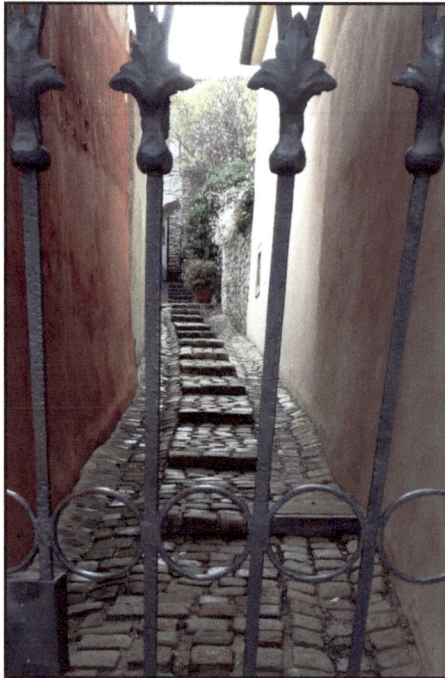

ISBN 978-1-912460-64-9

HIGH TATRAS 2009

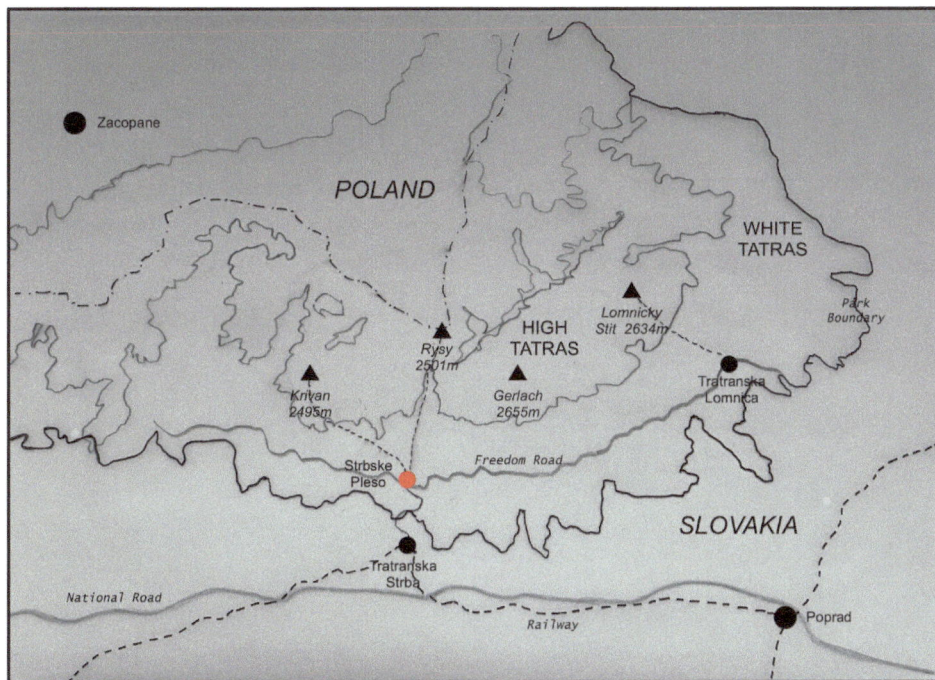

Bratislava

Monday 24 August 2009

Peter was a post-doctoral student and he and wife Paulina and their son Paul lived in our house in Cambridge for a few months in 2007.

Peter met us at Bratislava airport and drove us to their apartment, a renovated apartment block on the northern outskirts of the city. We are both tired having been to Andy and Meribel's wedding the day before, but we are woken by little Paul, known as Palko, at six am.

At breakfast in the kitchen we can see the Austrian border. Just over the river the summer palace of Maria-Therese, the Austro-Hungarian Emperor and a great plain stretching towards the Alps. After breakfast we drive to Paulina's parents where we are going to leave Palko.

Slovakia is green and hilly. The woods, that cover the hills like a quilt, meet the sloping fields in soft wavy lines. There is oak, ash, beech, hazel

Typical older housing block in Bratislava

and pine. There are bare harvested cornfields and recently cut hay meadows, with hay drying on wooden tripods. But there are no animals – no cows grazing in the meadows or sheep in the hilly patches between the trees. Peter says the EU has made pastoralism uneconomic, but I can't quite believe this.

It's all rather alien, very central European, something to do with living in a forest and coping with harsh winters. The villages we passed through getting here are quite different from English villages. Most of the houses are single storey with steeply pitched roofs. On the plains they are roofed in red tiles with cement render over block work. Here in the mountains the roofs are zinc sheet and the walls of stone and timber cladding. You have this feeling of autumn coming, seeing the harvest in and people enjoying themselves in the warm weather. The houses are arranged irregularly, sometimes with the gable to the street line. Many houses have large gardens with vegetable beds and fruit trees. Often there is large grass verge with large shade trees. The churches have spires with gilded cupolas. Everything seems orderly and tended. Peter says that in the 60/70s Czechoslovakia enjoyed the highest standard of living in Europe, certainly

Aerial view of a Bratislavan suburb

comparable to Britain. The country divided in 1993. Peter says it was a political decision. Maybe the Slovak politicians felt hard done by. But they now have close economic and cultural ties with the Czech republic, so it's not a problem. Peter says it combines features of both socialism and the market economy.

I'm constantly reading signs of the communism state into what we can see from the car. My impression was coloured by the cold war and the spy novels I read. Now it looks prosperous and pleasant.

We sit in the garden at Paulina's parents. Her father is a big man with huge strong hands. I'd noticed Palko's big hands that morning playing trains with him in his bedroom. The father is retired and a keen gardener. His plot is bare – he's harvested his main crop of garlic and onions. He has another larger garden where he grows potatoes and root vegetables. There are fruit trees heavily laden with peaches, apples and pears, vines and soft fruit bushes with different varieties of raspberry. He has a poly tunnel growing peppers. These are important in Slovak cuisine, which is close to Hungarian in style.

Every level surface in the house – the window ledges, shelves and tables

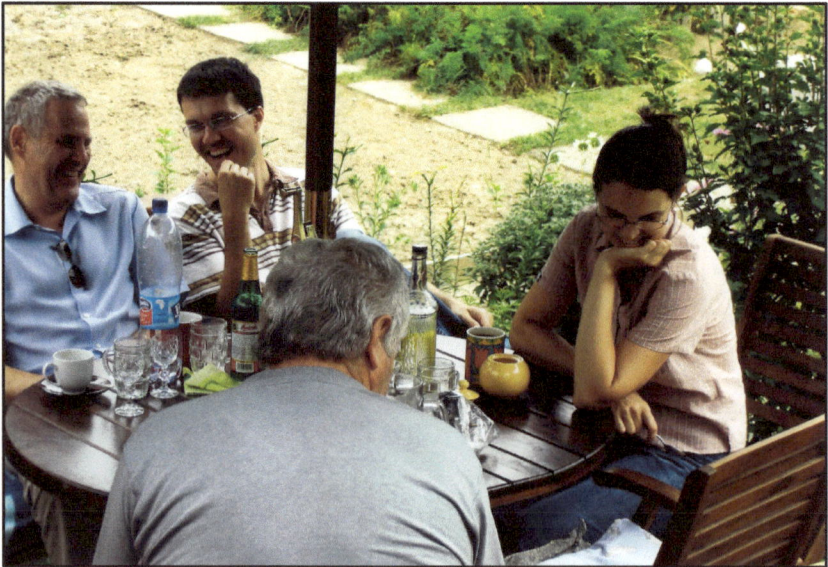

Breakfast at Paulina's parents' house

is laden with fungi of every description that are drying for winter storage. And the basement is full of root crops and apples.

We sit under an umbrella next to a homemade cast-iron stove on which he's cooking goulash. He is most insistent that we have an aperitif of homemade pear brandy. It's not actually homemade although it is from their own pears and made in the village. Like in England, it's illegal to distil your won spirits in Slovakia. We have beers with the goulash, which is pork and delicious, but feels too heavy at lunchtime. Palko has been bought a toy plastic drill but it doesn't work and so his grandfather takes it to pieces and fiddles around till he gets it to work and Palko goes around drilling everything in sight. We visit with Peter's parents in the next village. They have an older house and a larger garden, also with fruit trees. They serve us cake and tea and then we go back to Paulina's for a barbecue.

We fall asleep on the first part of the journey and wake on a twisting mountain road. It's quite narrow and Peter drives fast until we reach the main road where he's much more cautious and doesn't overtake rashly like some drivers.

We stop at a service station for a break. We can see a sharp mountain

Palko with his new toy drill

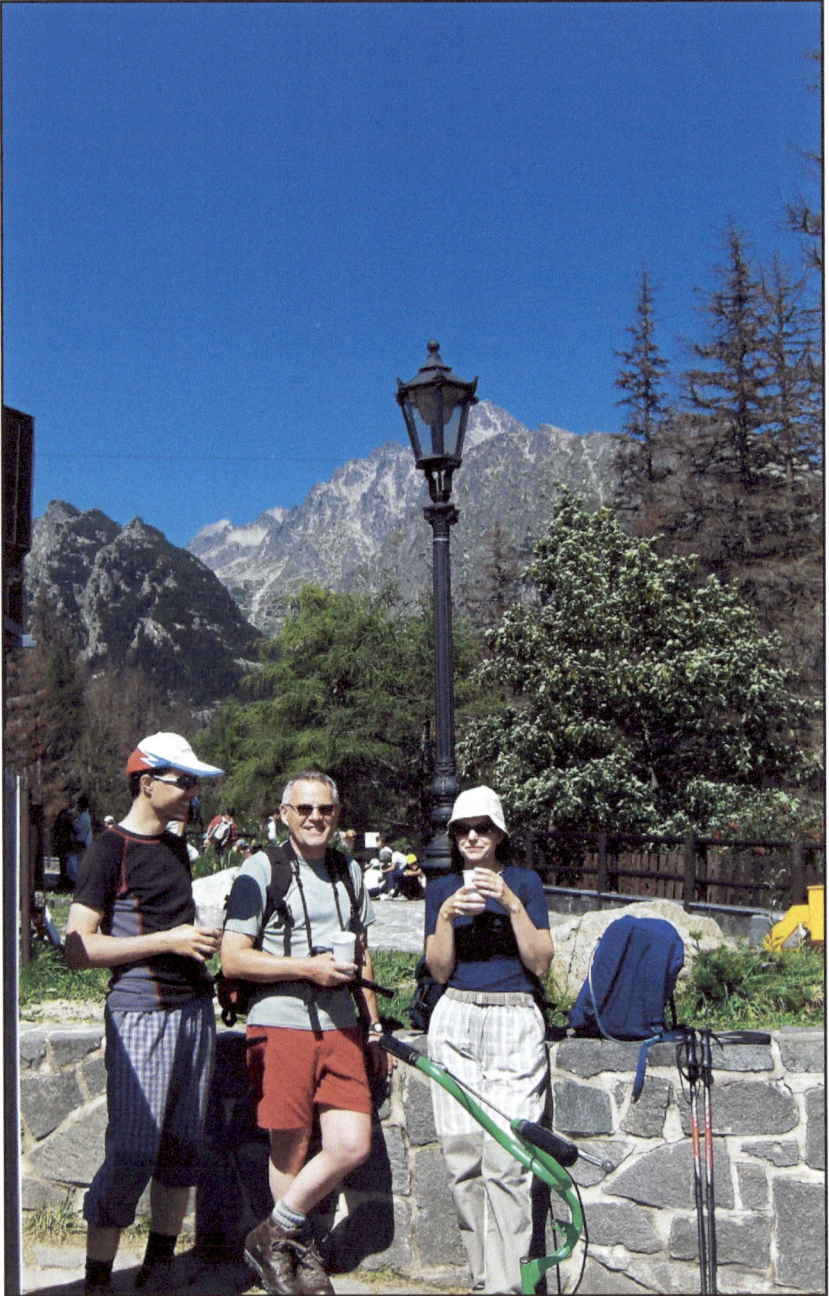

We arriove at Tatranska Strba

poking out of the clouds and I suggest that it might be Kriváň. It means crooked and I've seen photographs of it in the guidebooks. It's also the national symbol of Slovakia. Peter says no. But we consult the map and it seems I was right, it is Kriváň. It looks good and I want to climb it. But Scharlie and I are both feeling stiff and recovering from our operations. I had a new hip a year ago and although that is feeling strong at last, I pulled an Achilles tendon a fortnight ago running for a bus and can hardly walk. And Scharlie has an operation on her toe more recently and hasn't done any serious walking since. So we're a couple of old crocks.

We arrive at Tatranska Strba and, after ringing the custodian to ask for directions, find our hostel. It's vast and empty. We have adjoining rooms, sharing a toilet and shower.

Lomnicky Stit (2,634m)

Lomnicky Stit (2,634m)

Tuesday 25 August 2009

We wake reasonably rested at 6:30 wash and go for breakfast. The cook has made omelettes, but she's spread them with mustard and ketchup and I find it inedible. Never mind the bread is good. We pack and leave by 8:30 and walk to the rack and pinion railway that climbs up to the lake and hamlet at Štrbské Pleso There are lots of chalets hidden between the trees. They are well designed and individual. The gardens are fenced but left natural. But, as Paulina says, being in a forest they have no view. I wonder when they were built, who owns them now and how development is regulated. There must be strict controls in a national park.

We miss the way and lose time and miss the train by a whisker. Peter

Scharlie on the bridge over the river about Hrebienok

has almost reached the train as it pulls out. It's an hour wait till the next train, but it's pleasant in the dappled sunshine. There's a bench to sit. The train is full but we manage to find a couple of seats. I have my rucksack on my knee and suddenly realise that I don't have my binoculars. I remember I hung them on the end of the bench. The train is about to go. I leap up and ask the person next to the door to hold the train. They just giggle. I dash to the bench, expecting the train to leave and having to wait another hour. I find the glasses where I left them. Luckily the train doesn't start till I get back.

At Štrbské Pleso we buy tickets for the train that runs along the base of the mountain. We are going as far as Starý Smokovec mid way along. From here Scharlie and I opt to take the funicular up to Hrebienok while Peter and Paulina walk up the paved road. Apparently according to a sign the queen was here last year and the first part of the walk, which she did, is classed a fit for disabled. How appropriate!

We cross a stream by a bridge. The water is fast through large rocks. The children would love it. From here the path is more broken and rocky, but the ascent is gradual and we make reasonable time. For the first half

Traverse on broken ground to Skalnaté Pleso.

we are in trees and then it opens out as we traverse the last section to Skalnaté Pleso. A cable car comes up to the refuge here from Tatranská Lomnica. And from here a gondola goes up to the summit of Lomnický štít..

There is a small lake behind the refuge and we find a bench and have a late lunch with bread we've saved from breakfast and peppers from Paulina's father. Paulina wants to go to the top but the gondola is fully booked till Thursday. There is a chair lift to the saddle between Lomnický štít and Lomnický veža to the south. So we decide to take it and get what view we can. It's chilly on the lift and I'm glad I've got my fleece. From the col at Lomnicky Sedlo we traverse left to the summit. I looked back and wondered if it might be possible to climb the main summit from the col. it looks rather like the Aiguille du Midi. Paulina says we'd need ropes. With the binoculars I can see the route up the ridge to where it steepens into two or three pitches of climbing.

The Tatra to the west are in shadow from the setting sun. It's about five o'clock. We look through a notch in the ridge and can see a succession of spiky silhouettes receding into the distance with Gerlach, the highest, being

Looking west along the line of High Tatras

the most distant. There is a hanging valley with two tarns and a grassy moraine dome in the sunshine. Through the glasses I can see people and a large chalet. We have the apples and chocolate and relax in the late sunshine before starting back to the chairlift.

At Skalnaté Peter says that they'll walk down and we decide to join them despite my misgivings. I can see that the path down follows the ski slopes so I know what it will be like, broken and difficult. At first we follow our ascent path the dive off down to the left and the way becomes more difficult. There is a proper path through dwarf pine and gentians. On the ski slopes where the 2004 hurricane whipped through birch and poplar scrub is regenerating.

Finally we reach the midway ski lift and Scharlie and I opt to take the cable car down. We agree to meet Peter and Paulina in the railway station. We are turned back at the top to buy tickets in the shop. But they have just closed and the girl emerges and says it's too late. So we go back to the platform and sign language to the attendant and he lets us on for free. We have a beer while waiting and then almost miss our train arguing about not being able to use our senior citizens railcards. If we'd missed it

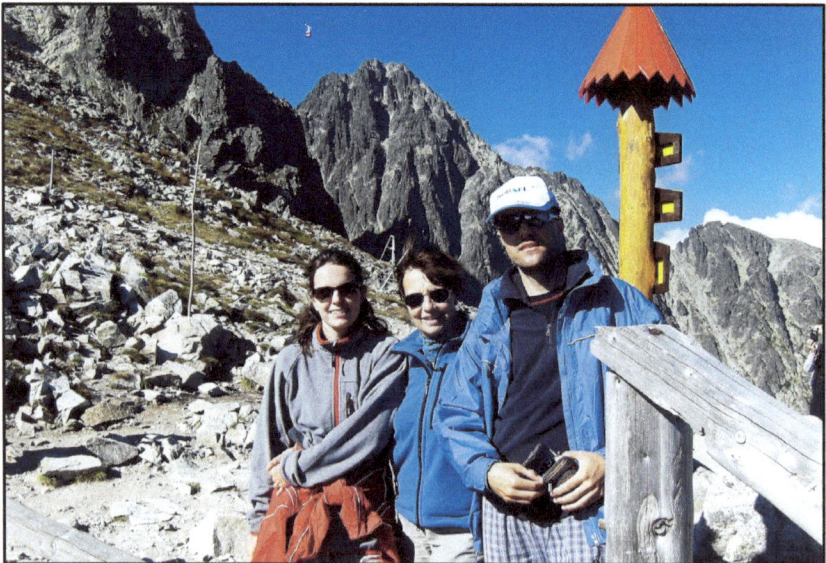

Start of chairlift to Lomnicky Sedlo

14

we would have had to wait another two hours. We don't have time to buy tickets for the rack and pinion in Starý Smokovec. We should have bought tickets right through. So we risk it and board without tickets. We doze and it's dark by the time we get off for the walk through the woods. I've brought the tiny head torch that Jess and Maddie bought me for Christmas and this is the first time I've used it. It's bright and strong and we find our way back easily.

They have left food for us in the chalet, soup and rice and veal, and we warm it up in the microwave. We get to bed at ten and sleep well.

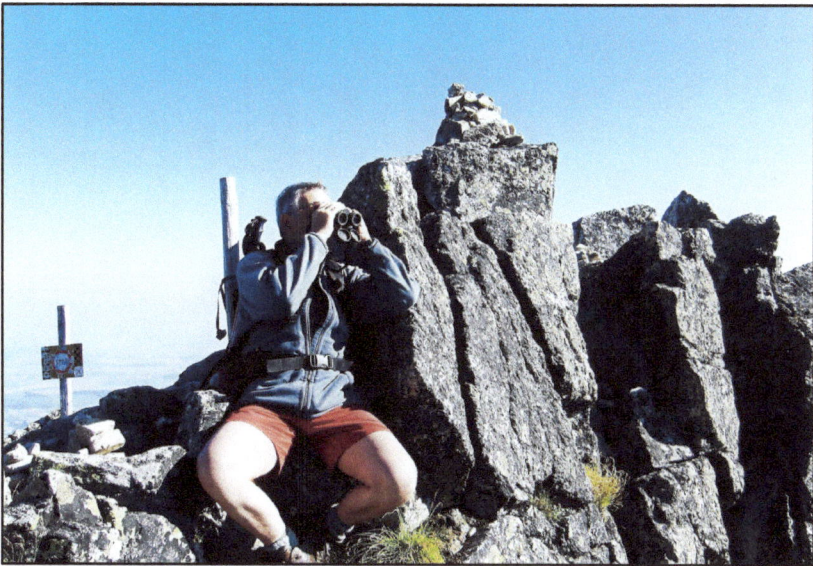

From the col at Lomnicky Sedlo we traverse left to the summit.

Cable car to the summit of Lomnický štít..

Return by cable car from the mid-way station

Kriváň (2,495m)

Wednesday 26 August 2009

Breakfast is better – eggy toast. But because Paulina asked the cook to serve ours without ketchup we don't get the ham and tomato either. We catch the rack and pinion in good time today.

Kriváň is our objective today. It's not the highest mountain in the Tatras, nor the hardest, but it is Slovakia's national symbol and appears of the Slovak Euro. We saw it from the main road looking dark and impressive. The name means crooked and the summit ridge curves round to form a cwm.

The first hour is an easy forest trail west from Štrbské Pleso. They are renovating the Kempinski hotel in front of the lake. The architecture is chocolate box Franz Joseph with steeply roofed towers and orange and

Kriváň (2,495m)

Hotel Patria, Strbske Pleso Lake

Amanita muscaria fungi (fly algaric)

green trim around the many windows. It's enormous. There must be at least a hundred rooms. The new extension is ultra modern grey stone and glass. The view of the lake with the mountains behind is quite spectacular. There is a ski jump and a striking timber triangular shaped hotel called the Patria.

There are lots of other walkers going our way and we overtake them and are overtaken by them as we wait for Scharlie to catch up. She likes to go slow at the start of the day and go at her own pace. We reach the junction where our forest trail meets the path coming up from the road. Now we are climbing steeply on a narrow rocky trail through pine forest. When it begins to open out Peter stops and we wait 40 minutes or so for Scharlie. My legs are sore but I'm doing alright. I feel much less strong than before the operation though.

It continues getting more open and levels off. There are large granite boulders and dwarf pine. There is a view into a deep green valley to our right and we can see small dots of people on the summit ridge. The path is paved with huge slabs like a staircase. I'm tired. My body feels leaden. It seems endless but you just have to keep putting one foot in front of the

The path opens out with granite boulders and dwarf pine

Path up Kriváň

other. We traverse left around the ridge to where another path comes up from the southwest. From the junction with this new path you can either scramble up scree direct to the ridge on the official path. We opt for the right hand path but miss our way a little. The ridge is stony and there are parts where you need your hands and have to scramble.

Finally we reach the summit cross and can see the view to the north and east along the line of the Tatras. I find a place to sit and Scharlie arrives and then Peter and Paulina. We have a leisurely lunch of peppers, bread and soft cheese I bought in the village. It's still clear but there are big cumulous clouds. A glider cuts through the air right above us. I change out of my shorts. This seems to be the thing to do as a girl also changes just near us.

It seems much longer than you expect on the way back. You can't quite believe it, remembering how tired you felt on the way up. The first part is tricky down exposed rocks. This is the part Paulina had trouble with on the way up. I keep to the left at first but there is a big drop into a hanging valley and so I work my way rightwards away from the edge.

The ridge curves away in front of us. Scharlie asks if I want to go back

Time to put on a fleece

Summit rocks

Summit of Kriváň

along the ridge or more directly down the scree run. I say I think that the ridge will be easier on my legs and more aesthetic. But Scharlie, always averse to going back the same way wants to try the scree. I know if I insist on going by the ridge she'll go off on her own anyway. I feel we should stay together so I start down. It's difficult and loose and jars your bones when you slip. It's put me in a bad mood, but we get down without mishap and traverse along a way to a point where the ridge way joins. We find a grassy knoll and settle down to wait half an hour or so for Peter and Paulina. They came by the ridge, but Paulina's foot is hurting from her new boots and that's why they're slower.

The middle section is the well-made path between dwarf pine. The view is great and unlike on the ascent you have time to enjoy it. Going up you have to concentrate on each step and narrow your focus to the next few yards. If you constantly looked up at where you were going or stopped to

Seems a long way back

gaze around you'd never get up. It's an exercise in concentration in which the desire to get to the top winds over the dull pain of aching thighs, tired limbs and painful breathing. There is a view back to the summit of our mountain and we find a heathery mound to sit and wait.

The final section through the forest has more ascent than I remember. We fill our water bottles at the 'dog kennel' pipe and finally reach the bottom at seven o'clock having taken 9 hours and twenty minutes with rest stops. There is a train at 8:10 and we go to the station bar and have beers and persuade the cook to do us meals. They close at 8 and catch the same train we want. So we have a rushed meal. We order fish fingers, chicken and mushrooms but they all look the same in a thick brown breadcrumb crust. A sleepy train journey is followed by a stumble through the forest in the dark.

Paulina on the exposed part of the descent

Delightful way-marking

Ski-jump at Strbske Pleso

Strbske Pleso Lake

Waiting for the rack and pinion train back

Rysy (2,511m)

Wednesday 26 August 2009

We wake later than usual, stiff from our exertions yesterday and Scharlie assumes we won't go the Rysy. I say there is still time. At breakfast Peter and Paulina are quiet and Scharlie feels frustrated and asks them about plans for the day. She suggests that Peter and I can do Rysy while she and Paulina find something easier. Peter asks if I want to do it and I say yes if my legs hold up. So we galvanise ourselves and sprint for the train.

We call at the mini-market again and I buy a large bottle of water to supplement my water bottle, as I don't want to get de hydrated. It's cloudier today but still looks ok. We set off along the road and then start up through the pinewoods. There is a swooshing noise. It's skiers on the ski jump running on an artificial plastic surface. It looks terrifying.

Buying supplies at the mini-market

Rysy (2,511m)

Trail up Rysy

Views of Rysy

We set a brisk steady pace and keep going until we reach a point where the blue and red routes join. Peter points out bags of onions waiting to be transported up the mountain to the refuge. They offer a reward of a mug of tea. Peter says he'll do it next time he comes. The vegetation thins. It's similar to yesterday's middle stretch. We cross two wooden bridges. At the second one I insist we stop. We have been going over an hour and I need a drink. We are off again after a couple of minutes. I check the map and see that our path should diverge to the right about now. Soon after we see a sign to Rysy. The main path continues up the valley while ours climbs steeply. Peter goes off fast and leaves me behind. This is the last I'll see of him till near the top.

The path zigzags up the hillside. It's hard work in the hot sun and I'm sweating with the effort. I can see a ramp traversing to the right across the cliffs. This is where the chains are. It's easy and the chains are largely unnecessary in these conditions apart from a smooth slab where stainless steel hoops have been let into the rock to make steps. I'm faster than other people on this section but they soon overtake me on the next steep bouldery section to the lake.

Chains next the summit

On the summit

Looking north towards Poland

I stop again briefly to have a drink and admire the view, then off again climbing steeply to a welcome sign on a rock and the final ascent to the refuge. It begins to spot with rain and I get my anorak out. By the time I reach the col it's raining hard. It's misty but I can see the way up easily by the lines of people descending. The rain has obviously driven them from the summit. I try and keep a look out for Peter thinking he must be on his way down by now. He wouldn't want to sit this deluge out waiting for me on the top. I'm head down when I hear his voice. I ask him if that's the summit we can see ahead but he says no, it's around the corner and that the hardest part is near the top. We arrange to meet back at the refuge and I press on.

The path goes over the ridge to the left and then steepens and becomes indistinct in a mass of boulders. It's very steep and you need to use your hands and scramble up. It's hailing now and the storm is so fierce that the water is pouring down the summit slabs like a river.

Finally I reached the top. A pretty girl smiles at me and I smile back. Then I realise her boyfriend is trying to take a photograph of her and I'm in the way. I asked her to take one of me with the view of Poland in the

Rest at the refuge

background. I stay about 10 minutes or so and the weather clears a bit and I get a good view.

The start down is steep and I have to take care not to slip. I almost go towards Poland as the way is marked red, just like the way up from Slovakia. The sun comes out on the way to the col and I feel good to have got to the top and my legs feel strong enough to get back I find Peter inside the refuge and we have bowls of delicious cabbage and sausage soup. It's incredibly revitalising.

While Peter orders I move to a table near the window with a bench seat. The man opposite says we met earlier and I recognise him and his partner. A father with two daughters arrives and wants me to move to make room for him, so I ask my new friend to explain I'm saving the place for Peter. The man is a bit huffy.

The couple show me a photograph they took of me and offered to send it if I give them my email. The man has a nice sense of humour and the girl smiles a lot. They did Krivan on Monday, and it rained hard, so he thinks the bad weather follows him. She is very friendly.

I'm feeling stronger after the food and a rest and Peter lets me set the

Nice friendly couple in the refuge

On the descent

Bridge crossing

pace and we go fast overtaking people. We're still only halfway down when the storm hits us again and the path quickly floods on the level stretches. We keep going fast. Peter says we'll stop at the picnic place where the paths diverge but there is nowhere to shelter so I wrap my wallet and map in my waterproof trousers and we bash on, plunging through the puddles and slipping on tree roots.

It's still drizzling when we reach Strbske Pleso and my boots are wet through. I can feel my such socks. squelching. Peter spots that the train is about to go and we run for it. I jog behind, hoping my tendon won't go again. As soon as we are on we both try and ring our spouses to check they're down. Luckily they are. I had visions of them waiting for us in the coffee bar bored out of their minds.

We are down much earlier than on previous days and have only taken six and three quarter hours including the stop at the refuge. Back at the refuge I empty my rucksack of water, wring out my socks and strip off the rest of my clothes and hang everything on the balcony. Then have a delicious hot shower and I change into dry clothes. Dinner is the usual soup, followed by a beef stew with dumplings with bread.

Rest breakk

Číž Spa and Bratislava City Centre

Friday 28 August 2009

We get up slightly more leisurely fashion and after breakfast wander around the institute trying to see where the owners huge panoramic vista of Krivan was taken from. There is a pasture and open hillside where they must have set up the camera.

I drop off to sleep on the journey. The mountains are covered in cloud and we can't get a view of Krivan and Rysy, so we go to Strbske Pleso to buy something for Palko, and Paulina finds a sheep's bell she thinks he like and Scharlie buys postcards.

We get onto the motorway and head for the spa. We buy two tickets and Scharlie and I get a discount. One side of the complex is the fun area with a huge pool with loungers at the sides where people can stretch out in the water. There's an old guy chatting up a young girl. There are chutes

Spa

and an oval pool with a current that carries people round in a circle. On the other side of the complex, there are the mineral pools.

The water is brown and the temperature of each pool is marked. The hottest is 37 degrees centigrade, nearly body temperature. Most of the pools have seats around the edge. There is a cascade In the middle, which massages your back and shoulders. We move from pool to pool sampling them all. After two hours, our muscles are feeling relaxed and a lot less stiff. It's sunny, but not too hot, although some people look like lobsters. I vow that I'll go swimming when we get back, but I don't know if I'll stick to it, as I don't really like swimming pools.

We get back into the car and set off for Bratislava. It's fantastically hot, 32 degrees centigrade, and at times the traffic is slow. Peter doesn't have air conditioning on fully and I'm in the front seat in the hot sun. We stop at a service station to buy coffee, crisps and water.

The first part of the journey is through a narrow valley by the side of a wide shallow river and we can see people rafting. There are ruined castles on the isolated granite outcrops. Peter says they date from 7th century Gran Moravia. Scharlie asks about Moravian missionaries, and Peter explains

Thermal pool and cascade

that two missionaries brought Christianity to Slovakia, or Moravia as it then was.

We reach Bratislava about six and find a parking place by the river below the castle. We wander into the Old Town starting at the central square. It's pedestrianised and as it cools its pleasant. We're feeling stiff from our exertions yesterday. We pass the American Embassy in the main street with its fencing and gatehouse and Peter says they plan to move because they feel it's not sufficiently secure. We come to an open plaza near the cathedral where Habsburg monarchs were crowned. There is a crown on the dome of the tower. There is a holocaust memorial and Paulina says that this used to be the Jewish ghetto, but that the communists cleared the area. Maybe the pogrom dates from the German occupation.

The British embassy is the first building on the next street. One of the city's motifs is bronze statues. We see Hans Christian Andersen, Andy Warhol and Napoleon; all have some connection with Slovakia or Bratislava. Near the local government offices, there is a WiFi area with people on the benches consulting their email on their laptops.

Back in Bratislava

Sitting with Napoleon

St Martin's Cathedral

Čumil bronze sculpture of sewage worker emerging from a manhole

British Embassy

In the main square there is a statue of Napoleon and a cannon ball still stuck in the town hall tower. We climbed to one of the city gates, it's still hot and we're feeling hungry, so we start back and Paulina chooses a Slovak restaurant. The waiter is quite a comedian and takes our photo. The meal is good and I tell stories about Ivan and writing his biography.

In the night, there is a huge storm and it doesn't get cool until 4am in the morning. Peter and Paulina, take us to the airport. It's small and friendly. We take off 40 minutes late Scharlie chats to a young Slovak who is going to Cardiff to do a masters. He describes how Czechoslovakia and Slovakia were split by Hitler, who promised the Slovaks their own state when he annexed Czechoslovakia. He said 40% of the people voted for the National Socialists, and Slovakia was a Nazi puppet state during the war. Clearly Slovakia has always been under the influence of powerful empires. Habsburg, Austro-Hungarian, Nazi and Soviet.

Dinner in a Slovak restaurant on our last evening

Hans Christian Anderson

Michael's City Gate

Helen in Bratislava on a CAR work trip in 2013

Maximilian Schokocafe Delikateso

New and old apartments

www.ingramcontent.com/pod-product-compliance
Lightning Source LLC
Chambersburg PA
CBHW042131080426
42735CB00001B/42